100 Reasons

to

Vote for

Republicans & Not Democrats

Written by: Gary G McDonald

Introduction

After reading through such an amazing book with about 200 pages in it; titled "Reasons to Vote for Democrats", which was a gag book. I've decided to publish my own book on why you should vote for Republicans.

Table of Contents

Acknowledgements

There maybe people out there that don't agree with some of the things I say in this book, but who gives a rat's ass. The Republican Party are known to be some tough ass politicians that don't ask for handouts and don't like to give out any like the Democrats. They despise Obama Care and rather Americans pay for everything they want, including health insurance. This book is dedicated to all those that believe in Making America Great Again, whatever that may mean to you.

ISBN: 9798352189481
Pillar to Post Publications

Chapter 1

Established in 1854

Power

Respect

Religious

Conservatives

Gary G. McDonald

Wealthy

11

Arrogant

Gary G. McDonald

Winners

13

Hate to Lose

14

Electable

Jerks

Gary G. McDonald

16

Egotistical

Methodical

Crazy

Supports Death Penalty

Gary G. McDonald

Believes in Private Healthcare

Jackasses

Gary G. McDonald

Stubborn

Relentless

Deal Makers

Don't back Down from a Fight

Gary G. McDonald

Number Crunchers

27

Tax Breaks

Gary G. McDonald

Stallers

Savages

Gary G. McDonald

Will go to Prison for their belief's

They have Zero fucks to give

Gary G. McDonald

Pro-Life

Against Gun Control

Gary G. McDonald

For Domestic Oil Exploration

35

Narcissist

Greedy

Risk Takers

Gary G. McDonald

Deportation

39

Capitalism

Keep Control of the House

41

Shrewd

attitudes

42

Insurrectionist

Their
Constituents
have flex

To the Point

Top of the totem Pole

Snobbishly

conceited

47

Political Ties on both Sides

Swagger

49

Presumptuous

Gary G. McDonald

Free Thinkers

51

Money

52

Power

Determined

Oath Keepers

G.O.P

Ambiguous

Facetious

58

Go Getters

Inconsiderate at Times

Black People used to be Republicans

Self Sufficient

62

Elite Division

63

Rule Breakers

Gary G. McDonald

Take No Prisoner Mentality

Cutthroats

Back door Dealers

Wall Climbers

Monument Builders

Leather Hearts

Gary G. McDonald

Chess Players

You Know What We'll Do!

Gary G. McDonald

God Complex's

Sometimes We Ain't Shit

Gary G. McDonald

Head Choppers

Bill Stallers

Gary G. McDonald

Ambitiously Courageous

Riddle Solvers

Gary G. McDonald

Paper Plane Throwers

We Take Shit!

Gary G. McDonald

Belligerent at Times

Born Leaders

Gary G. McDonald

Seat Takers

It Makes More Sense to Vote Republican

Loyalty

85

Strict Laws

Gary G. McDonald

Blunt

Old Fashioned

Gary G. McDonald

Tough on Crime

89

Tenacious

Bag Chaser

Pardons

92

About That Life

No Filter

Gary G. McDonald

Voting Enthusiast

Innovative

Gary G. McDonald

Space
Explorers

97

Gary G. McDonald

Control

99

They Brag Differently

We Have the Last Say. We Give a little, to Gain a lot.

Checkout My Other Books

Pillar to Post: A Felons Story

The New Man: Role Reversal

Unarmed 2032

Pillar to Post 2: The Wonder Years

Beamed In: We Came to Play

Handsome

How to Avoid Jail and Prison Survival Guide

Patches

The New Man 2: Origins

Buyers Are Liars: Untold Stories of Downlines

White Lies: 11 Days on the Run

Checkout More Books

Crayons Can Still Color

Step-By-Step Guide Easiest Way to Writing

The Insiders 2020: Technological Melancholy

Ordinary People

Patches 2: Fantasy Island & The Mask of Bali

Gray Hairs

The FRRC Experience

Autonomous: Crash Course

Gmcdonald480@gmail.com